Edward S. Curtis Chronicles

NATIVE
NATIONS

by Don Nardo

Content Consultant

Dr. Barbara Robins
Associate Professor
Department of English
University of Nebraska Omaha

Essential Library

An Imprint of Abdo Publishing | abdopublishing.com

abdopublishing.com

Published by Abdo Publishing, a division of ABDO, PO Box 398166, Minneapolis, Minnesota 55439. Copyright © 2018 by Abdo Consulting Group, Inc. International copyrights reserved in all countries. No part of this book may be reproduced in any form without written permission from the publisher. Essential Library™ is a trademark and logo of Abdo Publishing.

Printed in the United States of America, North Mankato, Minnesota
032017
092017

Cover Photo: Edward S. Curtis/Edward S. Curtis Collection/Library of Congress
Interior Photos: Edward S. Curtis/Edward S. Curtis Collection/Library of Congress, 4, 7, 9, 12, 14–15, 41, 47, 48–49, 53, 57, 62, 66, 70–71, 75, 77, 78, 83, 84–85, 86–87, 89 (top), 99, 100 (top middle), 100 (bottom left), 100 (bottom middle); Edward S. Curtis/The Miriam and Ira D. Wallach Division of Art, Prints and Photographs: Photography Collection/New York Public Library, 10–11, 20, 26, 45, 54, 59, 60–61, 65, 69, 90, 96, 100 (bottom right); Edward S. Curtis, 16; Charles Deering McCormick Library of Special Collections/Northwestern University Library, 25, 42–43, 72–73, 88, 89 (bottom), 100 (top left); Edward S. Curtis/Library of Congress, 28, 32–33, 34–35, 36, 38–39, 50, 100 (top right); Hein Nouwens/Shutterstock Images, 31; Scene from Cecil B. DeMille's The Ten Commandments, Photographs of the filming of Cecil B. DeMille's The Ten Commandments, PC-RM-Curtis, courtesy, California Historical Society, PC-RM-Curtis_546, 81; Archive Farms Inc/Alamy, 94

Editor: Melissa York
Series Designer: Becky Daum

Publisher's Cataloging-in-Publication Data

Names: Nardo, Don, author.
Title: Edward S. Curtis chronicles Native American cultures / by Don Nardo.
Description: Minneapolis, MN : Abdo Publishing, 2018. | Series: Defining images |
    Includes bibliographical references and index.
Identifiers: LCCN 2016962129 | ISBN 9781532110153 (lib. bdg.) |
    ISBN 9781680788006 (ebook)
Subjects: LCSH: Indians of North America--Portraits--Juvenile literature. |
    Curtis, Edward S.,--1868-1952--Juvenile literature. | Photographers--United
    States--Juvenile literature. | Photography in ethnology--Juvenile literature.
Classification: DDC 970--dc23
LC record available at http://lccn.loc.gov/2016962129

CONTENTS

CHAPTER ONE

Witness to a Piegan Ritual

Edward Curtis became well known for his portraits of Native American subjects, such as this portrait of Yellow Kidney of the Piegan tribe.

Thirty two-year-old photographer Edward S. Curtis's eyes widened at the magnificent sight that stretched before him. Mere minutes before, he had been on horseback crossing a stretch of open prairie in northern Montana. With him was magazine editor George B. Grinnell, a conservationist with a deep interest in American Indian life. The two white men had met two years before on a mountainside in Washington State and had quickly become friends.

From the start, Grinnell was impressed with Curtis's camera skills. The editor urged Curtis to put his talent to work capturing images of

American Indians. Curtis replied that he had indeed already thought about doing just that. "The idea dawned on him," Grinnell later recalled, "that here was a wide field as yet unworked. Here was a great country in which still lived hundreds of tribes."[1] Some of those groups, Curtis had said, "still retain many of their primitive customs and their ancient beliefs."[2] It would certainly be a great achievement, he added, to use photography to preserve what was left of those cultures. Today, the use of words such as *primitive* in relation to Native cultures is jarring and racist, but at the time, the two men considered themselves sympathetic friends to the tribal members they met and photographed.

Grinnell wanted to help his friend make up his mind about tackling such a grand project. To that end, he invited Curtis to go with him to Montana. There, Grinnell said, they would visit the Piegans, or Pikuni, one of the tribes of the

CRITIQUES OF CURTIS

Though he was well-meaning and a gifted photographer, several modern Native observers say Curtis too often tried to romanticize Native Americans. His goal, they explain, was to make them appear as the stereotypical "noble savage" of the past. This ignored the reality that their cultures were already changing. Some wished to adjust to modern American life. Others kept their traditions as best they could as the US government outlawed their religions and languages and separated them from their children in government boarding schools. "Curtis is attacked most often, and most legitimately," art historian Lucy Lippard writes, for failing to depict American Indian life and customs accurately. "His soft focus blurred what might have been improper details," she says. "He staged scenes, routinely retouched and faked night skies, storm clouds and other dramatic lighting effects. He erased unwelcome signs of modernity," such as clocks and early automobiles.[3]

The Piegan camp, 1900

Blackfoot Confederacy. Each summer they came together in a large camp. There they held an ancient religious ceremony called the sun dance. The US government had outlawed the ritual and most similar Native American religious expressions in an effort to stamp out tribal cultures, but the tribe defied the order. The curious Curtis hoped to witness that ritual, and in early summer 1900, the two men rode to Montana.

Take Plenty of Time and Smile a Lot

The two travelers crested the top of a low hill. Curtis described the experience of riding up to the camp: "Suddenly," Curtis later recalled, he and his companion "rode out in full view of [the Piegan] encampment and beheld a truly thrilling sight."[4] Curtis estimated there were more than 200 large lodges, or teepees.

Entering the camp, Curtis immediately became fascinated by Piegan culture. He found all the tribe's generations—from children to grandparents—living together in one village. Grinnell cautioned him to take plenty of time in getting to know the residents. He should also smile a lot to put the Piegans at ease. Curtis carefully followed this advice. He smiled almost constantly, and most of the villagers smiled back.

Curtis eagerly got to know White Calf, chief of the Piegans. That leader introduced him to other members of the tribe, who came to like and trust the young photographer. They told him about their lives and were even candid about their recent problems with hunger. Their main food source—the buffalo—was swiftly disappearing from the plains, they explained. As a result, a few years before, one-quarter of the tribe had died in a single winter.[5]

DO NOT SAY "CHEESE"

Some of Curtis's modern critics have pointed out that the smiles and laughter he reported did not come through in his photos of the Piegans and other Natives. Curtis is known to have posed his subjects to fit his conception of what "Indians" should look like. Indeed, "The common theme throughout Edward Curtis's portraits is stoicism," says Cherokee scholar and blogger Adrienne Keene. "None of his subjects smile. Ever." Yet,

> To anyone who has spent any time with Indians, you know that the 'stoic Indian' stereotype couldn't be further from the truth. Natives joke, tease, and laugh more than anyone I know—I often leave Native events with my sides hurting from laughing so much.[6]

Curtis wrote down nearly everything the Piegans told him. He also took numerous photos of both individuals and customs. White Calf said he would allow him to photograph almost anyone and anything he desired. The one exception was the sun dance ceremony itself. It was extremely private, the chief said, and must be observed only in person by selected guests.

When it came time for that sacred ritual to unfold, Curtis watched all of it closely. He also took careful, detailed notes.

Piegan women play an integral role in the sun dance.

According to Curtis, each year a woman of the tribe promised the sun she would build a lodge, in return for curing the illness of a family member. During the five-day ceremony itself, tribe members sweat in the lodge, made an offering of dried buffalo tongues to the sun, and sang and danced.

A Massive Undertaking

Curtis had been greatly impressed by everything he had seen at the Piegan camp. In particular, however, the sun dance ceremony deeply moved him. He called some portions of it "wild, terrifying" and "elaborately mystifying." He added, "I was intensely affected."[7]

Curtis was so inspired by the experience he made a fateful decision. He would devote several years of his life to documenting American Indian cultures. It appears his motivation for such a project was twofold. First, he had a genuine interest in Native cultures. Second, and perhaps more pressing, he worried that many Native nations and their cultures were fast disappearing and therefore must be documented before they were gone.

Curtis manipulated the background of this photo, taken during the day, to look like the night sky.

By today's standards, Curtis's belief in a vanishing Native society turned out to be both mistaken and a disservice to Native Americans. Native nations were not dying out. Thomas King, a writer of Cherokee and Greek descent, explains that when Curtis came along, the cultures were "merely changing from what [they] had been to what [they] would become next." Thus, Curtis "was looking for the literary Indian, the dying Indian," which was an "imaginative construct," King adds.[8]

As a result, Curtis tried hard to capture the American Indian of the past rather than the American Indian of the present and near future. He took boxes of clothes, wigs, props, and scenery, so he could make his subjects look "Indian" enough. And, as King explains, sometimes, "he would provide one tribe of Indians with clothing from another tribe because the clothing looked more 'Indian,' so his photographs would look 'authentic.'"[9]

Despite Curtis's many mistakes in dealing with American Indians, King cautions, people today should not "be petty and ignore the immensity of the project and the personal and economic ordeal Curtis undertook."[10] In fact, during his visit to the Piegan village, Curtis had no

Curtis's photos often show the cultural
practices that make each tribe distinct, such
as these Kwakwaka'wakw dancers.

notion the project would take him 30 years to complete. During that long period, he would

take between 45,000 and 50,000 photos.[11]

Those many pictures would come together with thousands of pages of Curtis's written

description. The resulting set of books would feature 20 large, leather-bound volumes.

Together, they would bear the title *The North American Indian.* As both a research project and

a publishing venture, it would prove to be nothing less than enormous. The *New York Herald*

would famously come to call it "the most gigantic undertaking since the making of the King

James edition of the Bible."[12]

"There is a part of me that would have preferred that Curtis had photographed his Indians

as he found them," King states. Still, "he spent his life photographing and writing about

Indians," in an enormous, well-meaning effort. "He died harnessed to that endeavor, and when

I look at his photographs . . . I am humbled."[13]

CHAPTER TWO

Becoming a Photographer

The most famous white photographer of Americans Indians, Edward S. Curtis, came into the world on February 16, 1868. His birthplace was a small house in the countryside near Whitewater, Wisconsin. Young Edward's parents, Johnson Curtis and Ellen Sheriff Curtis, struggled to make a living.

Not long before, Johnson had come home from the American Civil War (1861–1865) exhausted and penniless. For a while, he tried various jobs. But eventually he became a roving preacher for a local Christian group. The pay was low, so the family was poor. It was not

Edward Curtis self-portrait, ca. 1889

unusual for Edward and his siblings to go for weeks with only potatoes to eat. Those siblings included his older brother, Raphael, and his younger sister and brother, Eva and Ashel.

When Edward was young, the family moved to rural Cordova, Minnesota. There, Reverend Curtis made regular long trips visiting the widely separated members of his church. Edward often went along. Hiking and canoeing through the countryside imparted to the young man a strong love for the outdoors.

New Interests and Responsibilities

During this period, Edward developed another love that remained with him throughout his life, a love of photography. When his father returned from the Civil War years before, he brought home an unusual object: a camera lens he had found. Using that lens and some odds and ends he scraped together, Edward built a simple but workable camera. In addition, while still a teenager, he may have worked for a while in a photography studio in nearby Saint Paul, Minnesota.

In 1887, Johnson decided to look for new business opportunities in the nation's northwestern sector. He and Edward, then 19 years old, moved to the tiny town of Sidney, Washington Territory, situated across Puget Sound from the then-small city of Seattle. Ellen and the two younger children followed in the spring of 1888. They arrived to find Johnson in poor health, and he died only a few days later. The oldest son, Raphael, had already left home. So Edward assumed financial responsibility for the family.

In the next couple of years, Edward took on a number of unskilled, tedious jobs, including clam-digging and helping neighbors with chores. In 1891, however, he borrowed $150 from a local bank and bought part of a Seattle photography studio.[1] Not long afterward, he felt financially stable enough to court a longtime family friend, Clara Phillips. They married in 1892. And in the next several years they had four children, Harold, Beth, Florence, and Katherine.

EDWARD'S FIRST CAMERA

At the age of only 12 years, Edward built a workable camera. He utilized the lens his father had brought back from the Civil War. It had originally been part of a stereopticon, a device that projected photographic images on a screen or wall. To construct the camera, Edward followed directions he found in a popular photography book, *Wilson's Photographics*. The young man poured over the book's text, learning everything he could about the photographic process. The book even explained how to make prints, or finished photos on paper.

A clam digger of
Puget Sound

First Meetings with American Indians

By the mid-1890s, Curtis had built a reputation as Seattle's leading photographer. People of all walks of life came to the studio and posed for his cameras. His success brought him a degree of financial freedom, so at times he went outside the studio to capture images of things that interested him. Among his subjects were the region's spectacular mountains and ocean beaches.

On the beaches of Puget Sound, Curtis frequently encountered small groups of American Indians. Some caught fish, and others dug for clams. Seeing them practice some traditional customs fascinated the young photographer.

These locals were peaceful and friendly, which did not fit the bloodthirsty image Curtis had long held of American Indians. He had developed that distorted viewpoint as a child back in Minnesota. In books, he had read how bands of fierce Dakota warriors had attacked local white settlers a few years before his birth. Hundreds of whites had died and many thousands had fled their homes. As he remembered learning, "the night sky was red with flame" as fields and homes were scorched and destroyed.[2] The youthful Curtis also heard that the white authorities

THE DAKOTA WAR

In 1861, the Dakotas in Minnesota were suffering starvation. The harvest had been poor, and there was no game to hunt on the reservation. They were supposed to receive treaty money from the US government in exchange for giving up their traditional lands and living on the reservation, but the money had not come. Four young Dakota hunters killed five white settlers on August 17, 1862. They asked their village to protect them from retaliation, and members of the village decided to begin a war to reclaim their land. The Dakota soldiers attacked isolated farms as well as white traders and government officials, with up to 1,000 fighters taking part in the conflict. They killed approximately 200 people and took 285 hostage, but the Minnesota militia defeated them, and they surrendered on September 23.[4] A military trial sentenced 303 Dakota fighters to death, of whom 38 were executed by hanging.[5] Meanwhile, 1,700 Dakota people, mostly women and children, were put in camps by the US Army. Attacked by angry white mobs and facing hunger and disease, up to 300 died. By May 1863, the Dakotas and 2,000 Ho Chunks who had no part in the conflict were moved to a camp in South Dakota.[6]

had captured hundreds of Dakotas and executed 38 of them in Mankato, Minnesota, with the approval of President Abraham Lincoln. As a boy, he saw drawings of these men "hanging at the end of a rope." He later said, "All through life I have carried a vivid picture of that."[3]

Princess Angeline

In 1895, one local woman of the Duwamish (Dkhw'Duw'Absh) tribe, Kikisoblu, particularly caught Curtis's attention. An older woman, the local whites called her Princess Angeline. He learned she was the last living child of Chief Seattle, after whom the area's early white settlers had named their leading city. Several years before Curtis moved to the region, the

Duwamish had lost their ancestral lands to those settlers. And since that time, the remaining tribal members had eked out modest livings at best.

"The first photograph I ever made of Indians," Curtis later recalled, "was of Princess Angeline."[7] At first, she refused to allow him to capture her on film. But when he offered her money, she changed her mind. "I paid the princess a dollar for each picture I made," he remembered. "This seemed to please her greatly." And "she indicated that she preferred to spend her time having her picture made than in digging clams."[8]

Curtis led Kikisoblu from the beach to his studio in Seattle. Once inside, she started to loosen her colorful bandana and scarf. But he stopped her. Clearly he felt she looked more like an "authentic" American Indian when in her usual attire. This was the first of many instances in which he posed or provided costumes so his subjects would seem more "Indian" to him.

Unaware that his subject might find this offensive, Curtis politely insisted, "Just as you are."[9] Kikisoblu's worn wooden walking cane added to her image in Curtis's eyes as a colorful Indian character, and he asked her to clutch it during the shoot. The most famous shot he took of her shows her staring away into the distance. With a built-in scowl and a mass of wrinkles, her ancient-looking face reflects a long life marked by hard work and sorrow.

Journey to the Tulalip

Curtis had heard that other Duwamish dwelled in a remote area north of Puget Sound. So did members of another tribe, the Suquamish. That area, called the Tulalip, was one of the isolated reservations where the US government had forced most American Indians to live. There, they practiced most of their traditional customs.

Curtis began paying brief visits to the Tulalip and got to know one couple well. They described to him their beliefs and daily habits. Entranced, he watched them weave baskets from river reeds and collect shellfish from nearby beaches. He captured these activities in pictures for which he paid, as he had paid Angeline. For these

IMPROPER TERMS

It is true that Kikisoblu was the daughter of an American Indian chief. But the term *princess* assigned to her by whites was not rooted in Native American cultures. The idea of princes and princesses being part of a nation's royalty is strictly a European concept. So using that term to describe Kikisoblu is inaccurate and can be considered somewhat demeaning. Debbie Reese, an enrolled member of the Nambé O-Ween-Gé nation, reviews children's books about Native Americans. She points out other words that whites sometimes use improperly when describing Indians. "Don't use 'shaman' to refer to our healers," she says. "Native people use our own words for healers. Shaman is an outsider's word."[10] Other inappropriate terms she cautions people to avoid are *Indian brave*, *squaw*, and *papoose*.

Curtis's famous
photo of Kikisoblu,
also called
Princess Angeline

A woman of the Lummi nation, or the Lhaq'temish, who live in northern Washington and southern British Columbia

tribes, Curtis observed, "agriculture was unknown." This was not because they were ignorant of growing crops. Rather, it stemmed from "the ease with which food could be had from the sea."[11]

While the photographer was making these observations, in late May 1896 Kikisoblu died. The news truly saddened Curtis, and he was only one among many local whites who viewed the event as symbolic. As one of the last of the Duwamish, her passing seemed to mirror the looming loss of all American Indians he expected to happen. He started to see them as a vanishing race, and this planted in him the seed of an idea. Perhaps, he thought, his camera might preserve some of their cultures for future generations.

CHAPTER THREE

First Major Adventure

By 1898, Curtis's investment of time and money in the photography business had paid off well. Both the photographic community and the general public had come to recognize him for his American Indian photos. He had also gained a name for capturing with his camera lens the Northwest's many natural wonders.

Rainier's Imposing Majesty

One of those superb sights was Mount Rainier, located 60 miles (100 km) southeast of Seattle. An active volcano, it rises to the impressive height of 14,410 feet (4,392 m). Curtis loved both climbing

Besides his portraiture, Curtis also photographed majestic landscapes, including this Alaskan scene.

and photographing it. Most of all, he was captivated by the mountain's rapidly changing moods. In the words of Curtis biographer Timothy Egan, they include "the savagery of its storms," the energy and color of "its wildflower burst," and the "fog that wrapped the mountain in spooky silence."[1]

Whenever possible, Curtis escaped his studio and city life to photograph Rainier's imposing splendor. The chief instrument he employed for this task was a view camera, a device invented in the 1850s. It had two principal parts. The front section contained the lens and a hand-operated shutter to snap the individual pictures. Meanwhile, the rear section housed a holder for a large pieces of glass.

When the operator lined up a shot, the lens in front projected the image onto the glass in the back. There, the photographer moved the lens-holder forward or backward slightly to

THE INTERPLAY OF LIGHT AND DARKNESS

In scouting out and composing photos of nature, Curtis was always very careful to take into account the existing lighting. He knew that every visual scene contains a complex interplay of contrasts between sunlit areas and places in shadows. In an article he wrote for *Western Trail Magazine* in 1900, he stated: "In the mountains the morning is almost the only time the atmosphere is clear and free from the blue haze. Every crag and peak casts long shadows, causing the whole [view] to stand out in rugged grandeur. Good pictures are the result of long study rather than chance."[2]

achieve a sharp focus. He then replaced the glass with a sheet of slide film. Finally he snapped the shutter, thereby creating a negative, which he would later use to make positive prints.

Rescue on an Ice Floe

It was in the spring of 1898 that a chance event occurred on Mount Rainier that radically altered the course of Curtis's life. While climbing the mountain, he suddenly heard a human voice crying out "Helloooooooo!" Curtis asked where the person was, and the voice repeatedly said "Over here!"[3] The photographer followed these sounds and eventually came upon six men who were clearly stranded on a tall, dangerous ice floe.

After Curtis had rescued them, the embarrassed men admitted they were lost. These individuals turned out to have very impressive credentials. Among them was Clinton Hart Merriam, a founder of the National Geographic

Curtis used a camera similar to this. The accordion-folded bellows allowed the photographer a lot of control over the camera's focus.

Twenty-three scientists traveled with the
Harriman Alaskan Expedition, including
famous naturalist John Muir.

Society. Also present was Gilbert Pinchot, chief of the US Forest Service. Curtis was most

impressed by George B. Grinnell, founder of the Audubon Society and a noted white expert on

American Indians. The two men immediately saw they had some important things in common.

One was a fascination for American Indian cultures. Another was a shared worry that Native

nations and their cultures were steadily and tragically disappearing.

The men Curtis had rescued were grateful for his help. After visiting his studio and seeing

his work, they were so highly impressed by his photography skills they invited him to join

a major scientific expedition. Scheduled for the following year, 1899, it would explore and

document the landscapes and Native peoples of Alaska. The United States had purchased the

region in 1867, but it would not become a state until 1959. The journey would be sponsored

by the well-known railroad tycoon E. H. Harriman. Hence, it was called the Harriman

Alaskan Expedition.

A Deep Resentment for Whites

Curtis accepted the offer to be the official photographer of the celebrated expedition to

Alaska. The voyage—his first great adventure—began on May 30, 1899. The explorers' ship steamed northward, skirting the rugged, frozen Alaskan coast. Harriman's son, Averell, later recalled seeing "the great glaciers all around and hearing at intervals the boom from the icebergs breaking off."[4]

Curtis was no less awed by the grand scenery. A tireless worker, one of his hallmarks, he strove to capture those mighty vistas on film. "The summer days in Alaska are long," he later remembered, "and Mr. Harriman urged that I make use of all the daylight."[5]

Most of all, however, Curtis was concerned with photographing the local American Indians. Among the original inhabitants of the region were the Tlingit, Haida, and Yup'ik Native nations. He found the Native residents along the coast disliked the whites taking photos of them. In part this was because they deeply resented most white people, whom they viewed as intruders.

The reason for this attitude was plain to Curtis and his colleagues on the Harriman team. In the previous few decades, white explorers and settlers had devastated the local Native nations. These peoples had long subsisted on fishing and seal hunting. White settlers had largely taken over the fishing industry and built fish canaries all along the coast. This had

Curtis captured this image of four boys in the Aleutian Islands, the island chain that trails off the tip of Alaska westward.

badly disrupted the local people's lives.

As a result, when Curtis tried to snap photos of the people he saw, they sometimes turned their backs on his camera. Without consent, he captured a few images of Native families going about their daily tasks, including cutting up seal carcasses to obtain meat. Similar to most white people of that era, Curtis assumed he could intrude into American Indians' daily lives without asking first. Meanwhile, his subjects, unhappy about his presence but desiring to avoid a confrontation, just frowned a lot.

The "Abandoned" Village

In late summer 1899, the Harriman expedition began its return trip to Washington State. On the way down the coast, the ship stopped at Cape Fox, which lies a bit north of the border between Alaska and western Canada. There, the team came upon a Tlingit village. Not a person could be found, and the place appeared to have been abandoned.

Most members of the team assumed the residents were gone and began collecting artifacts from the houses. In the course of a few hours, they carted away masses of clothing, blankets, baskets, totem poles, and other objects. Curtis was appalled, as he felt his shipmates were out-and-out looting the place. The scientists and others who took these goods argued they were not stealing. Instead, they claimed they wanted to preserve the objects by exhibiting them in museums rather than letting them lie around and rot.

CAPE FOX

Suffering from smallpox, the people of Cape Fox had left their homes in 1893. More than 100 years later, their descendants felt the loss of their belongings keenly. A repatriation project collected many objects from museums around the country and returned them in 2001. A great-great granddaughter of Edward Harriman spoke about the significance of the day and her family's joy that the objects were returning home. She presented a quilt that had been in her own family for more than a century, which tribal elders accepted as a gift of friendship and reconciliation.

In Grinnell's mind, the seemingly deserted village was one of many signs American Indians

were in swift decline. He said of the Alaska Natives, "Perhaps for a while a few" of them might

retreat "to the Arctic to escape the contaminating touch" of white society. But that move

would not halt the American Indians' inevitable "extinction." Whenever two civilizations

clash, he warned, "the weaker people must be destroyed."[6] Curtis sadly agreed. He did not

realize time would prove this cynical, gloomy attitude about the Native nations and people

utterly wrong. At that moment, Grinnell suggested that the two of them journey to Montana

the following summer. There, Grinnell said, they would hopefully witness a major ritual: the

renowned sun dance of the Piegans.

Making a Photogravure

To make prints, or finished photos, from his negatives, Curtis often (though not always) used a process called photogravure. Invented in 1879, it produces prints that feature rich texture, with warm blacks and delicate shades of gray. The process begins by coating a metal plate with light-sensitive gelatin. One then exposes the plate to light shining through one's negative. Curtis's negatives looked like large black-and-white photographic slides. The image on such a slide has varying light and dark areas. And when light passes through the negative, it creates an image on the coated metal plate. Next in making a photogravure, the photographer treats the plate with mild acid, which eats away the gelatin. The places where it eats deepest appear darkest in the finished print. Conversely, the places where the acid eats away the least amount of gelatin appear lightest in the finished picture. When the plate dries, the photographer applies ink to it. Finally, he or she presses a piece of paper against it, creating the print. The last step was originally done by hand but later by machines.

In this photogravure by Curtis, showing a Washo woman, the acid ate away the least amount of gelatin in the light background areas. The darker sections resulted from the acid eating away much more of the gelatin.

CHAPTER FOUR

To Benefit Future Generations

Curtis's award-winning photograph *Homeward*

By the turn of the 1900s, Curtis had become one of the United States' leading photographers. His Seattle studio, where many white residents of the region had portraits done, was a major success. Furthermore, his photos of American Indians had begun winning national awards. In 1898, for example, the influential National Photographic Society accepted some of his pictures for a major exhibition. Among them were two of his shots of Kikisoblu. Another was *Homeward*, a photo of five men in a large canoe in Puget Sound.

All three pictures made the finals of the show's yearly contest among photographers, and *Homeward* won the exhibition's grand prize.

Joseph's Moving Story

Such recognition allowed Curtis to charge considerably more for his work. It did not occur to him to share part of the proceeds with the Native American subjects of those images. Now financially well-off, however, he was able to hire people to run the studio and take vacations.

That well-earned luxury allowed him to make the trip to Montana he and Grinnell had planned for the summer of 1900. There, the two men studied Piegan culture. They also witnessed the famous sun dance. The experience convinced Curtis that Native nations and their cultures were disappearing and must be preserved for the benefit of future generations. Thus, he later recalled, the Montana trip marked "the start of my concerted effort to learn about" American Indians and "to photograph their lives."[1]

Also influential to Curtis in choosing to pursue that enormous project was his photo shoot of the renowned Nez Percé leader In-mut-too-yah-lat-lat, widely known as Chief Joseph. In 1903,

Chief Joseph's photo session with Curtis yielded two iconic photos, both published in *The North American Indian*.

the photographer learned Joseph was in Seattle. A friend of Curtis's brought the chief to the studio to have a portrait done.

As were most people of that era, Curtis was familiar with Joseph's story. The Nez Percé, or Nimi'ipuu, had originally controlled a large region centered where Washington, Oregon, and Idaho come together. But in 1877, the US government ordered them to live on a tiny reservation in Idaho. Chief Joseph and other Nez Percé leaders refused to submit. In the summer of that year they led their people toward Canada. There they would be free of capture by US soldiers. Thousands of US soldiers pursued the band in a 1,400-mile (2,250 km) chase. The Nez Percé ultimately made it to within 30 miles (48 km) of the Canadian border before the soldiers caught up. To avoid major bloodshed, Joseph grudgingly surrendered. The words he spoke at that moment later became famous. "I am tired," he said. "My heart is sick and sad. From where the sun now stands, I will fight no more forever!"[2]

ONE OF HISTORY'S GREATEST MEN

Curtis's studio portraits of Chief Joseph were taken shortly before the famous leader's death. Many modern historians and art experts believe Curtis's photos of Joseph effectively captured the chief's ongoing feelings of sadness about his people's loss of their homeland. The chief had certainly expressed his sorrow in his famous surrender speech, made in 1877. The Nez Percé had suffered the loss of several chiefs, he said. Furthermore, "The little children are freezing to death," and the tribe lacked enough blankets and food. "My heart is sick and sad," he stated, and his fighting days were over.[3] Still, Joseph continued speaking out against the unjust manner in which US authorities treated his people. The government broke its promise to allow them to return to their ancestral home. In contrast, Joseph kept his own promise to remain nonviolent. His eloquent words advocating freedom, equality, justice, and simple decency made him a widely admired figure. Curtis, himself one of those admirers, said of Joseph, "I think he was one of the greatest men that had ever lived."[4]

Chief Joseph

74-07

Curtis in Washington, DC

Curtis reasoned that the aged Chief Joseph was nearing the end of his life. And after his death, his people, dwindling in numbers, would also pass away. More and more Curtis worried all American Indians would suffer the same fate.

Curtis realized that to preserve those cultures in words and photos would be extremely costly. "Will I be able to keep at the thing long enough?" he wondered. It was plain to him that "doing it in a thorough way is enormously expensive."[5]

Clearly, to fund the grand project would require the backing of wealthy and important people. To that end, Curtis decided to turn for help and advice to President Theodore Roosevelt himself. Roosevelt shared Curtis's worry that all Native Americans would pass away. He publicly lamented that Native Americans were "on the point of perishing."[6] At the same time, however, Roosevelt was working to speed up the breakdown of the Native nations, calling for the government to stop recognizing tribal affiliation and deal with each Native American individual separately. He believed whites should control the continent.

By luck, meeting with the president became possible when Curtis won another important photography award. In 1904, his studio portrait of a white Seattle girl was singled out for excellence by the renowned magazine *Ladies' Home Journal.* A noted artist, Walter Russell, soon transformed that image into a painting. Russell was also slated to paint portraits of Roosevelt's children and asked Curtis to shoot photos of them first.

In June 1904, therefore, Curtis traveled to the president's estate in Oyster Bay, New York. There he ended up doing stunning portraits not only of Roosevelt's children but of the entire family. These photos were published in *McClure's* magazine in July 1905.

In part because both Curtis and Roosevelt were outdoorsmen and loved the American West, they quickly became friends. Roosevelt called Curtis's American Indian photos "genuine works of art." The images "deal with some of the most picturesque phases of the old-time American life that is now passing away." The president went on to praise Curtis for having "the will and power to preserve" a "strange and beautiful and now vanishing life."[7]

A Gigantic Idea

Roosevelt did more than simply compliment Curtis on the quality of his photos. The president also promised his support for the upcoming grand project. That support took the form of an enthusiastic letter of recommendation. Creating a large set of volumes about American Indians,

FORCIBLY DISRUPTING TRADITIONS

During the late 1800s and early and mid-1900s, the US government and white society worked actively to disrupt Native American cultures. As open conflicts with tribes ended and most Native Americans were forced to live on reservations, their children were taken away to boarding schools. The purpose of these schools was to teach white culture to Native children and prevent them from learning about their own heritages. Children were forbidden from speaking their languages and were even given new names. Abuse and hardship were common. It is against this backdrop that Curtis lamented the "vanishing" cultures, without recognizing the role his own people played in actively trying to extinguish them. As Jerry Potts, of Blackfoot ancestry, explains, "A lot of the photographs show the traditional people in their traditional garb. . . . They weren't showing what Indian agents and governments and everybody else were doing to our people at the same time. The state that Indian communities were in was really terrible."[8]

Roosevelt said in the letter, would be a truly impressive piece of scholarship. Curtis's photos "stand by themselves," the president continued. Moreover, they possess both "wonderful artistic merit" and "value as historical documents."[9] Roosevelt told Curtis he was welcome to use the letter to approach prospective backers.

The first potential sponsor to whom Curtis showed the letter was one of the richest people in the world, business mogul J. P. Morgan. The two men met on January 24, 1906, and after looking at some of Curtis's pictures, Morgan agreed to help. In exchange for Curtis's publication of a set of books containing such photos, Morgan agreed to put up $75,000.[10] At the time, that amount equaled 250 times the yearly salary of an average American worker.

Exactly why Morgan gave Curtis the money is uncertain. More than anything, it may have been the photographer's boldness, a trait Morgan greatly admired. A newspaper article had recently called Curtis "an artist with the camera." He was about to carry out the "gigantic idea of making complete photographic and text records of the North American Indians."[11] At the time most people felt that completing such a huge task would be downright impossible. But Morgan disagreed. He was well known for saying, "I like a man who attempts the impossible."[12]

Curtis photographed members of Native nations from Alaska to the American Southwest, showing a huge diversity of cultures in visually stunning shots, such as this Navajo man in ceremonial clothing.

CHAPTER FIVE

In the Great Southwestern Desert

A Hopi woman prepares food. As Curtis explains in *The North American Indian*, "Piki is cornbread baked in colored sheets of paper-like thinness. The batter is spread on the baking stone with the bare hand."

Curtis's trip to Washington, DC, and New York had turned out to be an extremely fruitful one. He had met, photographed, and become friends with President Roosevelt. Curtis had also met with the wealthy J. P. Morgan, who had agreed to help fund the photographer's upcoming documentation project.

Curtis returned to Seattle in mid-April 1906. Immediately he began making plans for an extended trip to the American Southwest, particularly Arizona. There, he intended to study and photograph the Navajo (Diné), Apache (Ndee), and Hopi (Hopituh Shi-nu-mu) peoples. The information he planned to gather would kick off the enormous collection of research required for his multivolume set of books.

While still in Seattle, Curtis penned a letter to Grinnell to express his excitement about the upcoming project. Among other things, Curtis stated, it was vital that the work be done as quickly as possible. "You and I know," he went on, that "the Indians of North America are vanishing." Indeed, "there won't be anything left of them in a few generations. And it's a tragedy—a national tragedy." He added,

FIGHTING EXTREME WEATHER

While in Arizona, Curtis found extremes in the local weather sometimes made his work difficult. In an undated recollection, he writes:

"The rain pours down. What was an arid desert when you made your evening camp is soon a lake. Perhaps in the darkness of the night you have been compelled to gather your [equipment] and carry it to higher ground. Or perhaps it is a fierce wind striking your camp, and if strong enough it will either blow your tents to the ground or whip them to shreds."[2]

I can live with these people. [I can] get their confidence, understand them, and photograph them in all their natural attitudes. . . . I can start—and sell prints of my pictures as I go along. I'm a poor man but I've got my health, plenty of steam, and something to work for.[1]

Curtis Photographs Geronimo

Curtis looked forward to visiting the Navajo, Hopi, and Apache nations. Moreover, he believed that a recent experience had prepared him well for his research on the Apache. In late February 1905, while still in the East, he had photographed the famous Apache leader Goyathlay, widely known by the Spanish name Geronimo. The US commissioner of Indian affairs, Francis Leupp, had arranged the shoot. It took place at a government-run school for young American Indians, where Leupp brought Geronimo. Geronimo had been a prisoner of war since he surrendered to the US Army in 1886. But in time, he was allowed—always under guard—to attend various official and social events. According to

Pueblo writer Leslie M. Silko, in one instance he boldly told his white guards, "So you captured me. The Mexicans would have killed me!"[3] Then he looked directly into the camera lens and promised to continue resisting when he could. Curtis took several shots of the renowned Apache fighter. In the best-known of these images, Geronimo looks to his right, not into the camera. It is lost to history whether Geronimo chose the pose or Curtis directed him. The next day, Geronimo rode in President Roosevelt's inauguration parade with leaders from five other tribes. Each had come to Washington, DC, to advocate for their tribes with the president.

With the Apache

On June 1, 1906, three months after photographing Geronimo, Curtis arrived in Arizona. With him was his son Harold, then 12 years old. Also part of the team was Curtis's new assistant, William Myers, an expert researcher. In addition, Myers was adept at stenography.

For a few weeks, they lived among and studied the Apaches who dwelled on two adjoining reservations. The white visitors managed to compile a detailed overview of the cultures of local Native nations. Curtis later said that it included their "history, life and manners, ceremony, legends, and mythology."[4]

A SPIRIT UNBROKEN

Geronimo's fame sprang from his skilled and fierce resistance to foreign armies. In 1858, his wife, three small children, and mother were murdered by Mexican soldiers. That tragedy turned him firmly against soldiers in general, including US troops when they intruded into Apache lands. In the 28 years that followed his family tragedy, he and a small band of followers fought and killed both Mexicans and Americans. Geronimo became most renowned for his ability to evade capture. In his last few years of freedom, 5,000 US troops hunted him, one-quarter of the nation's standing army. Vastly outnumbered, he and his men finally surrendered in 1886. But in the years that followed his capture, Geronimo never lost his pride and defiant attitude. After photographing him, Curtis observed, "The spirit of the Apache is not broken. He has lost none of his cunning, craftiness or endurance. But he sees that the day of the war-path is no more."[5]

In popular culture today, people yell the word *Geronimo* when they are jumping from high places. This is only tangentially related to Geronimo himself. It likely began when a group of military parachutists saw a Hollywood movie about Geronimo. They yelled the word while jumping to show they were not afraid.

Curtis's portrait of Geronimo

Curtis also obtained numerous stunning photos of the Apaches. Memorable among them are *Apache Girl* and *Bathing Pool,* but the best known of the lot is probably *Before the Storm.* It shows four Apache riders with a stormy-looking sky looming above them.

Entranced by the Navajos

In early July it was time to move on to the Navajo reservation, lying farther north in Arizona. At this point, Curtis's wife Clara and their children Florence and Beth joined him. All three children were fascinated by the local culture. Navajo clothes, jewelry, and crafts were markedly different than those of the Puget Sound Native nations.

Also distinctly different were the settings in which the Navajos lived. There was a striking blend of vast, flat deserts and sandstone canyons with towering walls and spires. The Navajos grew crops and tended to sheep in and near the canyons. The family enjoyed their time with the Navajos. Curtis described them

WILLIAM MYERS'S GIFTS

While in Arizona, Curtis discovered that hiring William Myers had been a smart and fortunate move. A man being interviewed "would pronounce a seven syllable word," Curtis later recalled. Then "Myers would repeat it without a second's hesitation." It appeared to Curtis that the other man saw this ability as "magic," and "so it was to me." Curtis further remembered, "We might spend the early part of the night listening to the Indian dance-songs." Later, "as we walked back to the camp, Myers would sing them."[6]

Curtis rarely photographed smiling subjects, like this Navajo woman.

as people who "laughed inside and out."[7] Curtis himself was particularly moved by the beauty of Navajo jewelry and painting. "As the chief human touch of the great southwestern desert," he wrote, "the Navajo are the artist's joy."[8]

Pursuing the Snake Dance

In August 1906, Clara and the children returned to Seattle. Curtis and Myers then left the Navajos behind and traveled 100 miles (160 km) west to the Hopi reservation. The photographer had briefly visited the Hopis a few times before. He was already acquainted with one of the leaders, Sikyaletstiwa. Curtis and Sikyaletstiwa liked and trusted one another.

In fact, not long after Curtis arrived on the Hopi reservation, Sikyaletstiwa officially made him a fellow Hopi. Curtis received a Hopi name and underwent an initiation ceremony. Moreover, Sikyaletstiwa adopted him. "If you will call me father," the chief told Curtis, "I will call you my son."[9]

These events made it possible for Curtis to achieve his main goal in visiting the Hopis. That tribe had an ancient custom called the snake dance, which Curtis called "a dramatized prayer for rain."[10] Curtis had long desired to photograph the dance and describe it in writing and now managed to do both. Among the many pictures he took of it, *Spectators at the Snake Dance* stands out. So do *The Catcher* and *Picking Up the Snakes.* He also wrote a tremendously detailed account of the entire ceremony. These accomplishments alone made him consider his Southwestern adventure a resounding success. As modern biographer Timothy Egan points out, Curtis "had gone deep into the culture of a people that [white] Americans had never understood."[11]

MESSENGERS OF THE RAIN DEITIES

After studying the snake dance, Curtis explained why he thought the Hopis connected rain and snakes:

> [Among] the Hopi and many other American Indians, the symbol of lightning is a zigzag line, [also] the [widely accepted] picture of a serpent. From the similarity between the sinuous gliding of a snake and the broken course of a lightning flash came naturally the concept of serpents as messengers of the rain deities.[12]

The Hopis themselves agree about the meaning of the zigzag line. They also point to an oral tradition that tells the origins of the snake dance. In it, a young Hopi man becomes involved with a young woman who is one of the Snake People, each of whom can change into a snake at will. The young woman becomes pregnant and gives birth to a baby who, like herself, can transform into a snake. In the story, the snake dancers are the descendants of that child.

The Catcher shows a Hopi snake priest holding snakes during the dance.

CHAPTER SIX

In the Land of the Head Hunters

Curtis considered his photographs fine art, which shows in their composition, romance, and soft focus, as in this image of Piegan homes.

Curtis was well into his huge photography project when major problems with funding began taking a toll. First, the money originally borrowed from J. P. Morgan was not enough to pay for everything. Year after year, large amounts of cash were needed to pay for assistants, cameras, sound equipment, and publishing the finished books. As a result, Curtis had to devote increasing amounts of time to borrowing money.

Other major distractions plagued the work as well. One was the outbreak of World War I (1914–1918). It had adverse effects on the US economy, and sales of Curtis's books temporarily stopped. His marriage began falling apart. He and Clara had often been separated for long periods while he was away living with and studying American Indians. In addition, it appears she finally realized he would likely never be free from debt. As a result, bitter divorce proceedings dragged on from 1916 until 1919.

His Tale of a Vanishing Race

As his money troubles increased, Curtis believed it was essential for him to find new outlets to raise cash. One very original approach he devised was a multimedia event he called a Picture Musicale. He projected striking hand-colored slides onto a large screen in a concert hall. They portrayed aspects of daily life among various tribes he had photographed through the years. He also hired a small orchestra. It played a score inspired by music he had recorded for

STILL SEEKING FUNDING

The people who lent Curtis money were many and diverse. In addition to the initial $75,000, Morgan gave him separate loans of $12,500 and $5,000.[1] Other people Curtis borrowed from included telephone inventor Alexander Graham Bell and the kings of England and Belgium. Famous steel tycoon Andrew Carnegie and noted politician Gifford Pinchot also lent him money. Curtis's frequent searches for extra funding seriously distracted him from his project.

Images such as *The Three Chiefs* exemplify the stereotype of the "noble savage," an idealized concept of a man not corrupted by civilization.

the project. Backed up by the visuals and music, Curtis himself narrated a moving tale he had written. He called it "The Story of a Vanishing Race."

The highly inventive show opened at Carnegie Hall in New York City in the fall of 1911. In the months that followed, Curtis toured it to other concert halls in major cities, including Washington, DC. Both as art and live entertainment, it was a popular and critical success. The *New York Evening World* said that it transported the audience "into the wild, romantic life of the [Native American]." And the *Washington Times* called it a "pictorial and musical gem."[2]

Unfortunately for Curtis, however, his artistic triumph proved to be a financial failure. The show was extremely expensive to produce. In fact, its costs were so great that they surpassed the profits made from ticket sales. Thus, when the months-long tour ended, Curtis was deeper in debt than ever.

Compelling Subjects for a Movie

Still desperate for money, Curtis turned to an even more spectacular art form, the motion picture. At the time, movies were rapidly expanding in popularity. Moreover, films about American Indians were in high demand. Curtis wanted to cash in on these trends. So early in 1912, he created the Continental Film Company.

For his first film project, Curtis chose to reenact life among the Kwakwaka'wakw, or Kwakiutl, before contact with white civilization. The Kwakwaka'wakw live in southwestern Canada, in the northern section of Vancouver Island. Curtis decided to focus on them because they were "one of the most important" tribes on the Pacific coast, he wrote. "Their ceremonies are developed to a point which fully justifies the term dramatic." Their "houses are large and

skillfully constructed." In addition, their "ceremonial masks and costumes [are] far in advance of any other group of North American Indians."[3]

There was something else that made the Kwakwaka'wakw compelling subjects for a movie. There was a great mystique surrounding the tribe because various legends claimed they had once been headhunters and cannibals. For that reason, the film's title became *In the Land of the Head Hunters*.

To prepare for shooting, Curtis needed to learn as much as possible about Kwakwaka'wakw customs and beliefs. So in the summer of 1912, he journeyed to Vancouver Island and met with George Hunt. Half white and half Tlingit, Hunt had long lived among the Kwakwaka'wakw and spoke their language. Hunt found that most of Kwakwaka'wakw were delighted to help make the movie a reality. To that end, he organized them into various production work crews. Some Kwakiutl carved and painted totem poles, masks, and canoes, while others made costumes. All of these artifacts were authentic to the time prior to contact with whites. The actors were Kwakwaka'wakw, making it the first full-length film with an all–American Indian cast.

From Artistic Triumph to Financial Flop

Curtis completed *In the Land of the Head Hunters* in late November 1914. It was fast-paced and contained numerous exciting scenes. Featured were chases, sea battles, head-hunting raids, and a wedding. The plot was fictional. But as a 1915 magazine article pointed out, the film accurately captured Kwakwaka'wakw customs and daily life.

The reviews for the film were glowing. One critic called it "a supreme art achievement" and another said it was "a genuine sensation."[4] Once again, however, Curtis found himself saddled with a great artistic triumph that was also a commercial failure. Not long after the film opened, a financial dispute erupted between Curtis and the company he had hired to distribute the film to cities nationwide. When he sued, the court case dragged on and on. All

BEYOND THE REACH OF MOST AMERICANS

Curtis needed to almost constantly raise money to make his 20-volume series on American Indians a reality. In large part, this was because of the hefty size and high quality of the volumes themselves. At the time, in fact, purchasing the full set was far beyond the financial reach of ordinary Americans. First, the photogravure process Curtis used to make the finished photos was extremely expensive. Furthermore, the special paper on which the pages were printed was imported at great cost. Incredibly, buying the full set was then equivalent to acquiring an 8,000-square-foot mansion. The end result was that only 214 full sets had sold by the time Curtis published the twentieth volume in 1930.[5]

The wedding party arrives in *In the Land of the Head Hunters.*

the while, he was not allowed to show the film, so it never recovered its costs.

One positive outcome of making the movie was that Curtis had collected reams of data about the Kwakwaka'wakw. He subsequently used it in writing the text of the tenth volume of his 20-volume project about American Indians. Curtis still required money to produce the next ten volumes. And despite his first film's financial flop, he believed the movie business might pay off in other ways. So when the time seemed right, he headed for Hollywood.

Striving for Authenticity and Originality

Curtis strove to present the Kwakwaka'wakw accurately in *In the Land of the Head Hunters*. This attempt at authenticity was widely and loudly stressed in the advertising for the movie. One goal was to show American Indians differently than most other films of that era did. Those movies typically presented the common stereotypes, such as fights between cowboys and Indians and Indians wearing feathered headdresses and wielding tomahawks. None of these things appeared in Curtis's film.

In the more than a century since the film was made, various scholars, along with members of the Kwakwaka'wakw nation, have reviewed and critiqued the film and its authenticity. The overwhelming judgment is that it is perhaps Curtis's most accurate representation of Native Americans. In large part this is because he hired members of the tribe to design and produce the sets and costumes. Among them was Tsukwani, the wife of George Hunt who was also known as Francine Hunt, who manufactured stunning Kwakwaka'wakw clothing made from the bark of cedar trees. The film's plot, having twists and turns common in white dramas of the era, "was certainly devised by Curtis," scholars Brad Evans and Aaron Glass point out. However, they say, Curtis's Native assistants "helped him flesh out the action with culturally relevant—and acceptable—performances" and technical aspects.[6]

Curtis's attempt to be authentic was not the only aspect of the production that was unusual or original. He shot the movie completely on location in British Columbia, Canada, instead of Hollywood. It also had inventive moving camera shots. And some sections of it were in color, created in an early process in which artists carefully tinted the film frames by hand.

A man wears clothes made from cedar bark.

CHAPTER SEVEN

Completing His Vision

Curtis would continue blending his role as artist and cultural chronicler, as seen in *A Smoky Day at Sugar Bowl*, which features a Hupa man.

With great difficulty, during the 1920s Curtis managed to finish his grandiose project on the American Indians of North America. During this period, he worked in near obscurity. In part this was because most Americans had lost interest in Native Americans and their cultures. Further, by this time most of Curtis's major and famous allies were either dead or very old and retired. He could no longer count on their support and letters of recommendation. Without them he had difficulty getting libraries and educational institutions to buy his photos and books. In addition, Curtis regularly struggled to raise money. As a result, he constantly worked on a strict budget.

Curtis and Cecil B. DeMille

Some of the badly needed funds came from Curtis's photography studio. In 1919, he had lost his original studio to his wife as part of the divorce settlement. That same year, however, he and his daughter Beth established a new studio in Los Angeles, California. Beth thereafter ran the business. That allowed Curtis to spend large amounts of time producing his American Indian photos and books.

Curtis needed to supplement the money his new studio made. So he took advantage of a convenient geographic fact: the proximity of Hollywood, the nation's film capital, to Los Angeles, where he lived. With his solid experience in filmmaking, he reasoned he could make some decent extra money photographing movies.

Curtis knew that motion picture photography took two forms. One consisted of shooting still photos of actors and movie sets, images that would be used to publicize various films. For instance, a film company paid him to take some publicity stills of Elmo Lincoln. Handsome and well-built, Lincoln was the first onscreen Tarzan.

A similar job came along in approximately 1920. Renowned film director Cecil B. DeMille was creating a huge screen spectacle, a silent film version of *The Ten Commandments*, which would be released in 1923. Curtis would shoot still photos of the production.

In addition, DeMille asked Curtis to operate a motion picture camera. That same year, Curtis worked as a second unit cameraman on *The Ten Commandments*. One of the large-scale scenes he shot was of the Israelites' flight from the Egyptian pharaoh. Another depicted dozens of Egyptian chariots chasing after them.

Documenting Distinctive Customs

Curtis spent only a few days, or occasionally a few weeks, on such film shoots. Most of his time was occupied with studying and photographing

Scene from *The Ten Commandments*, photographed by Curtis

Native nations and their people and cultures for his grand project. To that end, in 1922 he traveled to northern California and southern Oregon to photograph the region's tribes. His daughter Florence accompanied him as his general assistant. Also aiding Curtis in the ongoing research was his trusty assistant Myers. Their intent was to feature Hupa (Natinixwe), Yurok (Olekwo'l), the Klamath tribes (Klamath, Modoc, and Yahooskin), and other local Native nations in the project's upcoming thirteenth book. For the fourteenth volume, they planned to study the Cahto, Wailaki, and Pomo nations, as well as several other groups.

KLAMATH DIET

Curtis discovered the Klamath people of northern California enjoyed a diet rich in meat and fish. They hunted and ate deer, elk, bears, and beavers, for example. Other animals they consumed included rabbits, porcupines, foxes, raccoons, gophers, skunks, and even mountain lions, coyotes, and bats. The Klamaths were also avid fishers. Curtis wrote that they caught salmon, trout, and other types of fish "with hooks, in nets, or by spearing. There were two kinds of hooks: [one was] a straight, double-pointed bit of [deer-bone], to the middle of which the line was attached by means of sinew and pitch."[1]

Curtis found that several of these peoples had a number of unique customs. For example, Hupa dancers wore the bright red scalps of woodpeckers on their heads. Meanwhile, as Curtis recorded, the Yuroks refused to speak directly to dogs because they feared those canines might talk back. Another distinctive Yurok custom was burying their dead near the closest river with their heads pointing upstream.

A Klamath man in the forest

Members of the Yurok tribe also told Curtis they deeply respected redwood trees. Along with the other facts Curtis picked up when visiting the tribe, this has been authenticated by later generations of Yuroks. One of their tribal websites states, "Our traditional stories teach us that the redwood trees are sacred living beings. Although we use them in our homes and canoes, we also respect redwood trees because they stand as guardians over our sacred places."[2]

Curtis witnessed men of the Shasta people, another northern California tribe, dancing. "Twenty to thirty men would stand in a row," he wrote. Then they would "sing the war song." At the same time, they would strike "the ground with the right foot. And two young men with eagle-feathers in the hair and eagle-bone whistles in the mouth would dance and leap about in front of them." Now and then they would expel a big burst of air and shout "Pah, pah!"[3] Curtis also visited the Pomo people, whose homeland was located north of San Francisco, California. In his opinion, their most striking custom was making extremely high-quality woven baskets.

Nunivak

In the five years that followed, Curtis devoted the same time and energy he had with the Native nations of California to other Native peoples. This allowed him to create and publish volumes 15 through 19. To do the research for the last volume, in the summer of 1927 he traveled to Alaska. His goal was to capture life among the people of the remote island of Nunivak. He had heard they were still largely separate from and unchanged by white civilization.

The team initially stopped at the town of Nome, lying above the Arctic Circle. From there, in good weather it was a three-day boat trip to Nunivak. But the vessel encountered high winds and heavy seas. So the voyage through the freezing Arctic took nine days. The weary travelers reached Nunivak on July 10, 1927.

Curtis was delighted with the island's inhabitants, finding them "happy and contented." He attributed that fact to their being "unspoiled" by outsiders. "I have found a place where no missionary has worked," he remarked.[4] The team stayed on Nunivak for 16 days. During that interval, as usual Curtis took photos and jotted down information about his subjects. In turn,

This image, identified only as boys in a kayak in Nunivak, appears in Volume 20.

by day they learned what they could about him. Each evening many of them paddled their kayaks out to his anchored boat and watched and spoke with him.

Curtis published volume 20 in 1930. In its introduction, he described his feelings at that victorious and proud moment. There was a sense of fulfillment, he wrote, at having completed "thirty years of research." He continued, "Great is the satisfaction the writer enjoys when he can at last say" to his friends and supporters, "It is finished."[5]

AN ALTERED VIEW

Curtis's effort to emphasize traditional American Indian cultures also led him to alter some of his photos while processing them. For instance, it was not unusual for him to remove modern-style objects such as suspenders, umbrellas, and clocks from those images. This was a common practice of anthropologists at the time. A well-known example is his photo *In a Piegan Lodge*. The original image shows two Piegan men sitting on the ground, a clock visible between them. Curtis later retouched the picture, skillfully eliminating the clock.

A number of later Native observers have found Curtis's tendency to eliminate such objects both overly controlling and offensive. "He was a fan of doctoring images [and] erasing signs of 'modernity,'" Cherokee writer Adrienne Keene remarks. "His images created a false authenticity from which contemporary Indian artists struggle to break free."[6]

The clock was erased in the retouched version of this image, *bottom*.

CHAPTER EIGHT

From Last Years to Epic Legacy

In October 1927, after his voyage to the Arctic island of Nunivak, Curtis arrived in Seattle. His plan was to immediately move on to Los Angeles. But just before he boarded his train, the Seattle police arrested him. They told him that his ex wife, Clara, had pressed charges against him for failure to pay alimony during the previous seven years.

One of Curtis's famous images shows Navajo riders in Canyon de Chelly, Arizona.

Curtis Goes to Court

For the next few days, Curtis appeared in court three times to defend himself. There, he explained to the judge that he simply lacked the money to make alimony payments. His daughters Beth and Florence testified on his behalf and confirmed that fact.

The dispute then turned to Curtis's project, *The North American Indian.* Clara claimed it could potentially produce substantial profits. So the judge asked him how much he expected to make from selling the 20 books. Curtis replied that he would surely make nothing. The reason, he explained, was that he was deeply in debt throughout the many years he was creating it.

This reply confused the judge. If the books lacked the potential to make money, he said, why had Curtis worked so hard to complete them? Curtis's answer revealed a great deal about his character and personal motivations. "Your honor," he told the judge, "it was my job. The only thing I could do which was worth doing." The huge project had been "a sort of life's work," Curtis went on. And he "was duty bound to finish."[1]

It is unclear whether Curtis's statement contributed to the final court ruling. What is more certain is that the judge pointed out that the original alimony agreement could not be found.

Based on that, he dismissed the case. The charges against Curtis were dropped, and he was free to go.

Out of the Public View

Curtis now found himself at a pivotal moment in his life. For close to four decades he had been constantly preoccupied with creative work. He had also been a widely-known public figure. With his American Indian project completed, however, his life changed dramatically. For reasons that are somewhat unclear, in 1930 he fairly suddenly dropped out of public view for a period of two years.

To this day, no one knows exactly where Curtis was during that period. Some modern scholars suggest he may have been in a hospital because he was increasingly bothered by physical ailments. He had driven himself hard for many years and now suffered from both

CURTIS'S PHOTOS IN THE LIBRARY CONGRESS

The originals of Edward Curtis's photos rest in various archives around the United States. The largest collection of his images—more than 2,400 in all—rests in the Library of Congress, in Washington, DC. The library acquired them from 1900 through 1930, while Curtis was still alive and in the process of copyrighting them. After he died in 1952, his work was largely forgotten. Most of the original photos not in the Library of Congress collection languished in a basement of New York's Morgan Library. They became popular again when Curtis was "rediscovered" by the artistic world in the 1960s and 1970s.

Curtis self-portrait, 1940

exhaustion and depression. Furthermore, he had sustained a number of injuries during his wilderness travels.

In addition, some current experts on Curtis's life think his relentless financial problems seriously contributed to his depression. Desperate for money, in 1935 he sold most of his American Indian–related photos, metal plates, and books for a mere $1,000.[2]

Despite his money problems, Curtis had to support himself. One source of income came from his on-and-off work in the three photography studios his daughter Beth now ran. Another temporary job came from his old friend Cecil B. DeMille. In 1936, DeMille hired Curtis to shoot stills and motion picture film for *The Plainsman,* starring Gary Cooper.

In the decade that followed, Curtis's health problems worsened. In 1946, he accepted Beth's invitation to live with her on the small farm she and her husband owned near Los Angeles. Six years later, on October 19, 1952, Curtis died of a heart attack in Beth's farmhouse. He was then 84 years old and both penniless and unknown to most Americans.

Curtis often did not record his subjects' names, but recently tribal historians have been working to identify them. Curtis called this man "Chief of the Desert" instead of his name.

A Supreme and Unmatched Achievement

Following his passing, Curtis left behind an enormous legacy. It belongs not only to American Indians, but also the entire American public. But few people realized that legacy even existed until much later. Curtis died in near obscurity. By the 1950s his epic project, *The North American Indian*, had been largely forgotten by the vast majority of Americans.

In the 1970s, however, a major revival of public interest in Native nations and their histories and cultures began and is still ongoing. That trend brought Curtis's work once more to light. Historians, art critics, members of American Indian tribes, and the American public at large all marveled at his astonishing photographs. Especially passionate was praise for *The North American Indian*. That immense written and photographic account of American Indian cultures was now seen as a supreme and unmatched achievement. Art historian Christopher Cardozo called it "the most ambitious publication ever undertaken by a single man."[3]

Several of Curtis's modern admirers have tried to explain the importance of his work. Some applaud the beauty of his photos. These, they say, captured all aspects of American Indian cultures. Many modern members of Native nations have publicly recognized his contribution to recording their cultures. Pulitzer Prize–winning Kiowa writer N. Scott Momaday is one. For Curtis, he states, "The camera was truly a magic box. [It was] a precision instrument that enabled him to draw with light and transcend the limits of ordinary vision. [It enabled him] to see into the shadows of the soul. It is not by accident that he was called by his American Indian subjects 'Shadow Catcher.'"[4]

Momaday goes on to call Curtis "an American treasure."[5] Other experts say the treasure Curtis mined lies mostly in his incredibly detailed historical accounts of American Indian cultures. Curtis "preserved for future generations a crucial area in American history," says Cardozo. He "provided an opportunity to understand key aspects of the Native American experience." Moreover, Cardozo explains that Curtis wonderfully captured his subjects'

CURTIS AND NATIVE IDENTITY

Many decades after his death, Curtis is still praised as an uncommonly talented photographer. He is also remembered for his work to preserve American Indian cultures. However, some modern experts have criticized him. During the early 1900s, many Native peoples worked to adapt to white American culture. Curtis's critics frown on his consistent emphasis of the American Indians' older identity as so-called noble savages. This approach, they say, made their struggle to modernize harder.

Furthermore, some critics say, Curtis did not try to shape that older identity for the Native Americans' sake. Rather, he did it to create images of Indians that white people would buy. "I would put forth the assertion that Curtis' work is ultimately about [the] White Man, not indigenous people," photographer Larry McNeil writes. "Curtis's photographs are telling a story strictly from the standpoint of [the] White Man, plain and simple. It's a romanticized Western story that has little to do with reality."[6]

physical beauty. He also recorded for posterity their humanity and strong spiritual dimension. Therefore, Cardozo concludes, the "essence of this enduring legacy can be described simply as 'Beauty, Heart, and Spirit.'"[7]

The Native nations and the cultures Curtis photographed are bright and vibrant in the modern world more than 100 years later.

PHOTOGRAPHING NATIVE NATIONS

1. **"Princess Angeline"**

   Edward Curtis's first Native American images included portraits of Kikisoblu, commonly referred to as Princess Angeline.

2. **Piegan Sun Dance**

   Watching the Piegan sun dance helped inspire Curtis to begin his enormous project of photographing and writing about Native cultures.

3. **Roosevelt portraits**

   Meeting and photographing President Theodore Roosevelt and his family opened doors for Curtis to find funding.

4. **Chief Joseph portrait**

   Curtis is perhaps best known for his portraits, such as this one of Chief Joseph (In-mut-too-yah-lat-lat).

5. *In the Land of the Head Hunters*

   Curtis's film *In the Land of the Head Hunters* features the Kwakwaka'wakw tribe and was perhaps his most accurate representation of a Native culture.

6. *The North American Indian*

   Curtis worked on the 20 volumes of *The North American Indian* for 30 years.

Quote

"It was my job. The only thing I could do which was worth doing."

—Edward Curtis, describing his book *The North American Indian*

GLOSSARY

affiliation
An official attachment or connection to an organization or group.

alimony
Money a person is legally bound to pay to his or her spouse following a divorce.

anthropologist
A scientist who studies the origin, behavior, and development of humans.

Arctic Circle
An imaginary line of latitude located about 66.5° north of the equator. Most land masses and seas lying above the Arctic circle are very cold through much of the year.

commissioner
A government representative in an area or department who often has administrative and judicial powers.

credentials

References.

mogul

An important or powerful person.

second unit cameraman

On a movie set, a camera operator who shoots various secondary scenes on the orders of the cinematographer, or primary cameraman.

stenography

The process of using shorthand to take notes or write letters as someone dictates them.

stereotype

A widely held but oversimplified idea about a particular type of person or thing.

tycoon

A rich and usually important and well-known person.

Selected Bibliography

Cardozo, Christopher. *Edward S. Curtis: One Hundred Masterworks*. New York: Prestel, 2015. Print.

Davis, Barbara A. *Edward S. Curtis: The Life and Times of a Shadow Catcher*. San Francisco: Chronicle Books, 1985. Print.

Egan, Timothy. *Short Nights of the Shadow Catcher: The Epic Life and Immortal Photographs of Edward Curtis*. New York: Mariner, 2013. Print.

Makepeace, Anne. *Edward S. Curtis: Coming to Light*. Washington, DC: National Geographic, 2002. Print.

Further Readings

Adam, Hans Christian. *Edward S. Curtis*. Cologne, Germany: Taschen, 2012. Print.

Scherer, Joanna. *Edward Sheriff Curtis*. London, United Kingdom: Phaidon, 2008. Print.

Truer, Anton. *Everything You Wanted to Know about Indians but Were Afraid to Ask*. Minneapolis: Borealis, 2012. Print.

Waldman, Carl. *Atlas of the North American Indian*. New York: Facts on File, 2009. Print.

Websites

To learn more about Defining Images, visit **abdobooklinks.com**. These links are routinely monitored and updated to provide the most current information available.

For More Information

For more information on this subject, contact or visit the following organizations:

LIBRARY OF CONGRESS
101 Independence Avenue SE
Washington, DC 20540
202-707-5000
https://www.loc.gov/pictures/collection/ecur/

The largest single book collection in the world, the Library of Congress houses a collection of Curtis's photos, which can be viewed in person or online.

MORGAN LIBRARY AND MUSEUM
225 Madison Avenue at 36th Street
New York, NY 10016
212-685-0008
http://www.themorgan.org

The facility began as a place to house the private library and collections of J. P. Morgan, who financed part of Curtis's huge project on the Indians. It contains the vintage first complete 20-volume set of Curtis's masterwork, *The North American Indian.*

SMITHSONIAN MUSEUM OF THE AMERICAN INDIAN
Fourth Street & Independence Avenue SW
Washington, DC 20560
202-633 1000
http://nmai.si.edu/

This magnificent museum dedicated to Native American cultures contains one of the most extensive collections of Native American arts and artifacts in the world—approximately 825,000 items in all—among them a large number of Curtis's famous photos of American Indians.

SOURCE NOTES

CHAPTER 1. WITNESS TO A PIEGAN RITUAL

1. Timothy Egan. *Short Night of the Shadow Catcher: The Epic Life and Immortal Photographs of Edward Curtis*. New York: Mariner, 2013. Print. 43.

2. Ibid. 43.

3. Lucy L. Lippard. Introduction. *Partial Recall*. By Lucy L. Lippard and Suzanne Benally. New York: New Press, 1992. Print. 25.

4. Edward S. Curtis. *The North American Indian*. Vol. 6. Norwood, MA: Edward S. Curtis, 1911. 13. *Northwestern Library Digital Library Collection*. Web. 19 Jan. 2017.

5. Timothy Egan. *Short Night of the Shadow Catcher: The Epic Life and Immortal Photographs of Edward Curtis*. New York: Mariner, 2013. Print. 47–48.

6. Adrienne Keene. "Smiling Indians and Edward S. Curtis." *Native Appropriations*. Adrienne Keene, 22 Feb. 2011. Web. 19 Jan. 2017.

7. Barbara A. Davis. *Edward S. Curtis: The Life and Times of a Shadow Catcher*. San Francisco: Chronicle, 1985. Print. 31.

8. Thomas King. *The Truth about Stories: A Native Narrative*. Toronto, ON: House of Anansi, 2003. Print. 34, 37.

9. Ibid. 36.

10. Ibid. 37.

11. Christopher Cardozo. "Biography." *Edwardcurtis.com*. Cardozo Fine Art, 2017. Web. 19 Jan. 2017.

12. Barbara A. Davis. *Edward S. Curtis: The Life and Times of a Shadow Catcher*. San Francisco: Chronicle, 1985. Print. 55.

13. Thomas King. *The Truth about Stories: A Native Narrative*. Toronto, ON: House of Anansi, 2003. Print. 37.

CHAPTER 2. BECOMING A PHOTOGRAPHER

1. Barbara A. Davis. *Edward S. Curtis: The Life and Times of a Shadow Catcher*. San Francisco: Chronicle, 1985. Print. 18.

2. Anne Makepeace. *Edward S. Curtis: Coming to Light*. Washington, DC: National Geographic, 2002. Print. 20–21.

3. Ibid. 21.

4. "Camp Release." *The US-Dakota War of 1862*. Minnesota Historical Society, n.d. Web. 19 Jan. 2017.

5. "The Trials and Hanging." *The US-Dakota War of 1862*. Minnesota Historical Society, n.d. Web. 19 Jan. 2017.

6. "Forced Marches and Imprisonment." *The US-Dakota War of 1862*. Minnesota Historical Society, n.d. Web. 19 Jan. 2017.

7. Anne Makepeace. *Edward S. Curtis: Coming to Light*. Washington, DC: National Geographic, 2002. Print. 29.

8. Ibid.

9. Timothy Egan. *Short Night of the Shadow Catcher: The Epic Life and Immortal Photographs of Edward Curtis*. New York: Mariner, 2013. Print. 15–16.

10. "An Interview with Debbie Reese." *Rate Your Story*. Rate Your Story, 18 Nov. 2014. Web. 19 Jan. 2017.

11. Timothy Egan. *Short Night of the Shadow Catcher: The Epic Life and Immortal Photographs of Edward Curtis*. New York: Mariner, 2013. Print. 19.

CHAPTER 3. FIRST MAJOR ADVENTURE

1. Timothy Egan. *Short Night of the Shadow Catcher: The Epic Life and Immortal Photographs of Edward Curtis*. New York: Mariner, 2013. Print. 23.

2. Barbara A. Davis. *Edward S. Curtis: The Life and Times of a Shadow Catcher*. San Francisco: Chronicle, 1985. Print. 21.

3. Ibid. 25.

4. Anne Makepeace. *Edward S. Curtis: Coming to Light*. Washington, DC: National Geographic, 2002. Print. 36.

5. Ibid. 37.

6. Ibid. 40.

CHAPTER 4. TO BENEFIT FUTURE GENERATIONS

1. Gilbert King. "Edward Curtis's Epic Project to Photograph Native Americans." *Smithsonian.com*. Smithsonian Institution, 21 Mar. 2012. Web. 19 Jan. 2017.

2. "Chief Joseph." *New Perspectives on the West*. West Film Project and WETA, 2001. Web. 19 Jan. 2017.

3. Ibid.

4. Anne Makepeace. *Edward S. Curtis: Coming to Light*. Washington, DC: National Geographic, 2002. Print. 49.

5. Ibid. 59–60.

6. Ibid. 49, 69.

7. Ibid. 63.

8. Pedro Ponce. "The Imperfect Eye of Edward Curtis." *Humanities* 21.3 (May/June 2000). *neh.gov*. Web. 19 Jan. 2017.

9. Anne Makepeace. *Edward S. Curtis: Coming to Light*. Washington, DC: National Geographic, 2002. Print. 68–69.

10. Ibid. 71.

11. Ibid. 63.

12. Christopher Cardozo. "Biography." *Edwardcurtis.com*. Cardozo Fine Art, 2017. Web. 19 Jan. 2017.

CHAPTER 5. IN THE GREAT SOUTHWESTERN DESERT

1. Anne Makepeace. *Edward S. Curtis: Coming to Light*. Washington, DC: National Geographic, 2002. Print. 46.

2. Barbara A. Davis. *Edward S. Curtis: The Life and Times of a Shadow Catcher*. San Francisco: Chronicle, 1985. Print. 48.

3. Leslie M. Silko. Preface. *Partial Recall*. By Lucy L. Lippard and Suzanne Benally. New York: New Press, 1992. Print. 9.

4. Barbara A. Davis. *Edward S. Curtis: The Life and Times of a Shadow Catcher*. San Francisco: Chronicle, 1985. Print. 46.

5. Anne Makepeace. *Edward S. Curtis: Coming to Light*. Washington, DC: National Geographic, 2002. Print. 61.

6. Ibid. 91.

7. Timothy Egan. *Short Night of the Shadow Catcher: The Epic Life and Immortal Photographs of Edward Curtis*. New York: Mariner, 2013. Print. 130–131.

8. Ibid. 92–93.

9. Anne Makepeace. *Edward S. Curtis: Coming to Light*. Washington, DC: National Geographic, 2002. Print. 93.

10. Edward S. Curtis. *The North American Indian*. Vol. 12. Norwood, MA: Edward S. Curtis, 1922. 135. *Northwestern Library Digital Library Collection*. Web. 19 Jan. 2017.

11. Timothy Egan. *Short Night of the Shadow Catcher: The Epic Life and Immortal Photographs of Edward Curtis*. New York: Mariner, 2013. Print. 134.

12. Edward S. Curtis. *The North American Indian*. Vol. 12. Norwood, MA: Edward S. Curtis, 1922. 155. *Northwestern Library Digital Library Collection*. Web. 19 Jan. 2017.

CHAPTER 6. *IN THE LAND OF THE HEAD HUNTERS*

1. Timothy Egan. *Short Night of the Shadow Catcher: The Epic Life and Immortal Photographs of Edward Curtis*. New York: Mariner, 2013. Print. 216–217.

2. Anne Makepeace. *Edward S. Curtis: Coming to Light*. Washington, DC: National Geographic, 2002. Print. 121.

3. Edward S. Curtis. *The North American Indian*. Vol. 10. Norwood, MA: Edward S. Curtis, 1915. xi. *Northwestern Library Digital Library Collection*. Web. 19 Jan. 2017.

4. Timothy Egan. *Short Night of the Shadow Catcher: The Epic Life and Immortal Photographs of Edward Curtis*. New York: Mariner, 2013. Print. 239.

5. Christopher Cardozo. *Edward S. Curtis: One Hundred Masterworks*. New York: Prestel, 2015. Print. 25–26.

6. Brad Evans and Aaron Glass. "In the Land of the Head Hunters: Significance for Film History." *Rutgers School of Arts and Sciences*. Rutgers, the State University of New Jersey, 2017. Web. 19 Jan. 2017.

CHAPTER 7. COMPLETING HIS VISION

1. Edward S. Curtis. *The North American Indian*. Vol. 13. Norwood, MA: Edward S. Curtis, 1924. 169. *Northwestern Library Digital Library Collection*. Web. 19 Jan. 2017.

2. "Yurok History and Culture." *Yuroktribe.org*. Yurok Tribe, 2006. Web. 19 Jan. 2017.

3. Edward S. Curtis. *The North American Indian*. Vol. 13. Norwood, MA: Edward S. Curtis, 1924. 107. *Northwestern Library Digital Library Collection*. Web. 19 Jan. 2017.

4. Barbara A. Davis. *Edward S. Curtis: The Life and Times of a Shadow Catcher*. San Francisco: Chronicle, 1985. Print. 74.

5. Edward S. Curtis. *The North American Indian*. Vol. 20. Norwood, MA: Edward S. Curtis, 1930. xvii. *Northwestern Library Digital Library Collection*. Web. 19 Jan. 2017.

6. Pedro Ponce. "The Imperfect Eye of Edward Curtis." *Humanities* 21.3 (May/June 2000). *neh.gov* Web. 19 Jan. 2017.

CHAPTER 8. FROM LAST YEARS TO EPIC LEGACY

1. Barbara A. Davis. *Edward S. Curtis: The Life and Times of a Shadow Catcher*. San Francisco: Chronicle, 1985. Print. 74.

2. Ibid. 77–78.

3. Christopher Cardozo. "Biography." *Edwardcurtis.com*. Cardozo Fine Art, 2017. Web. 19 Jan. 2017.

4. N. Scott Momaday. Foreword. *Sacred Legacy: Edward S. Curtis and the North American Indian*. By Christopher Cardozo. New York: Simon, 2000 8. Print.

5. Ibid. 10.

6. Larry McNeil. "First Light, Winter Solstice." *Larry McNeil Photography*. Larry McNeil, 21 Dec. 2011. Web. 19 Jan. 2017.

7. Christopher Cardozo. *Edward S. Curtis: One Hundred Masterworks*. New York: Prestel, 2015. Print. 27.

INDEX

About the Author

Historian Don Nardo has published numerous books about American history, including several on Native American histories and cultures. In addition, his study of Depression-era photographer Dorothea Lang's famous photograph *Migrant Mother* was nominated for eight Best Book of the Year awards. Nardo, who also composes and arranges orchestral music, lives with his wife, Christine, in Massachusetts.